BABY BUBBLE WRAPS

designed by Anne Halliday

Wrap that baby in bubbles prettily perfect pampering for the wee one in your life.

Leisure Arts, Inc.
Little Rock, Arkansas

Wavy Strips

Size: 38 1/2" x 51 1/4" plus fringe

MATERIALS

Sport weight yarn,
6 oz white
10 oz lilac
10 oz lime

Note: Photographed model made with Red Heart® Soft Baby® #7001 White, #7588 Lilac and #7624 Lime

Size G (4 mm) crochet hook (or size required for gauge)

GAUGE

2 repeats = 10 1/4"

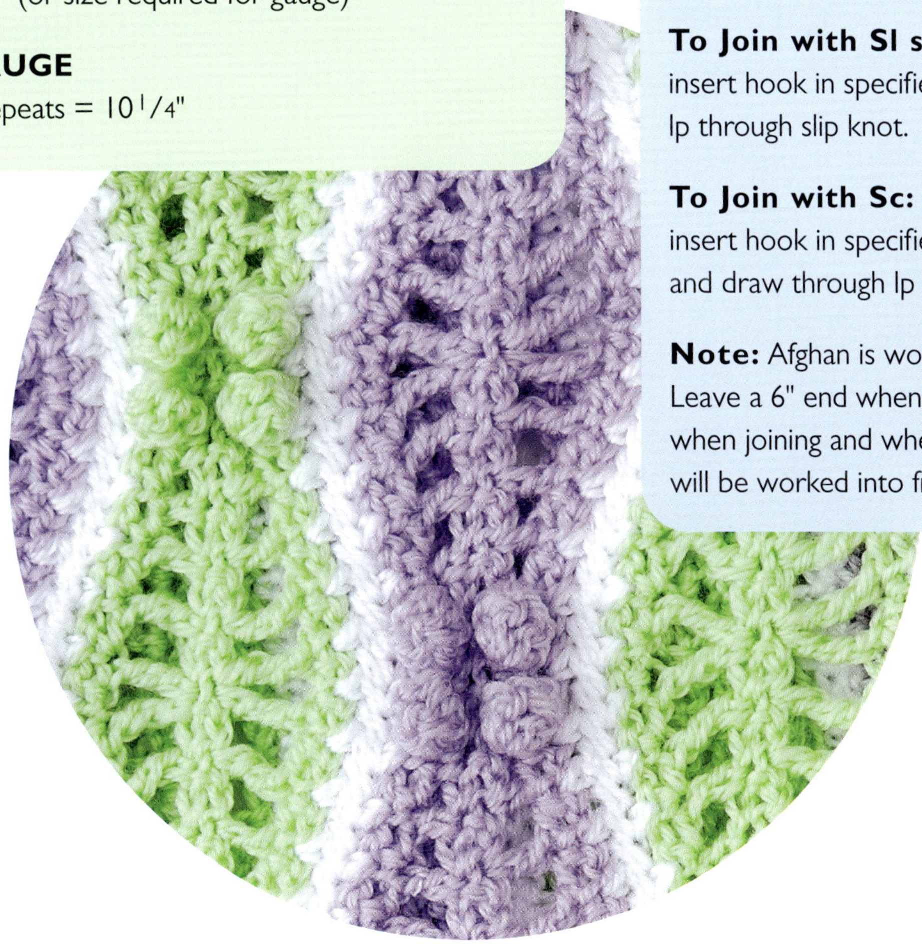

SPECIAL STITCHES

Cluster (CL): Ch 4, sc in 2nd ch from hook, 2 dc in next ch, sc in last ch (4-st row made); fold row in half from right to left, sl st in single lp at edge of first sc made: CL made.

V-st: (Tr, ch 1, tr) in specified st or sp.

To Join with Sl st: Place slip knot on hook, insert hook in specified st and draw up a lp, pull lp through slip knot.

To Join with Sc: Place slip knot on hook, insert hook in specified st and draw up a lp, YO and draw through lp on hook and slip knot.

Note: Afghan is worked in lengthwise rows. Leave a 6" end when starting foundation chain, when joining and when finishing off. These ends will be worked into fringe later.

Instructions

Strip A (make 9)

First Half

With lime, ch 202.

Row 1 (right side): Sc in 2nd ch from hook; ch 1, skip next ch, sc in next ch; *ch 1, skip next ch, hdc in next ch; ch 1, skip next ch, dc in next ch; ch 1, skip next ch, tr in next ch; ch 1, skip next ch, V-st in next ch; ch 1, skip next ch, tr in next ch; ch 1, skip next ch, dc in next ch; ch 1, skip next ch, hdc in next ch; ch l, skip next ch, sc in next ch**; (work CL, skip next ch, sc in next ch) twice; rep from * across to last 18 chs; rep from * to ** once; ch 1, skip next ch, sc in last ch: 31 sc, 20 hdc, 20 dc, 40 tr, 18 CL and 92 chs; ch 1, turn.

Note: Loop short piece of contrasting yarn around last sc made to mark as right side and top edge.

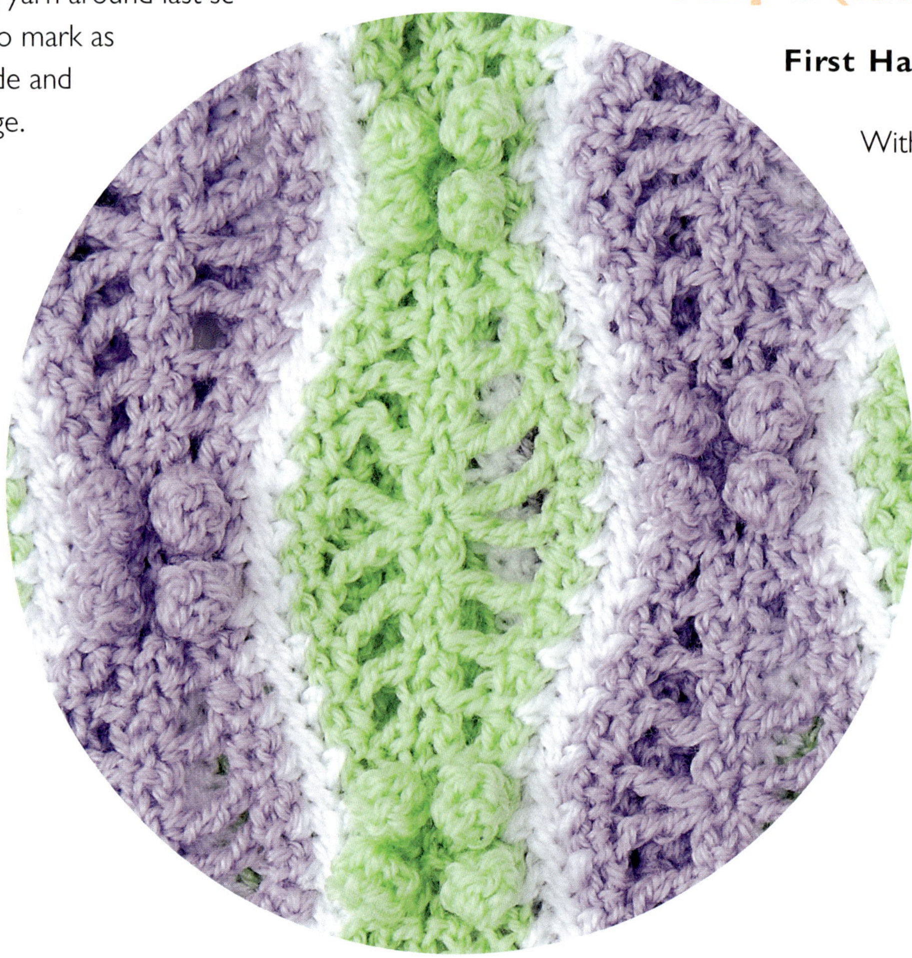

Row 2: Keeping CL on right side, sc in first sc; (ch 1, skip next ch, sc in next st) 5 times; ch 1, sc in next ch (not in ch-1 sp); ch 1, sc in next tr; *(ch 1, skip next ch or CL, sc in next st) 10 times; ch 1, sc in next ch; ch 1, sc in next tr; rep from * across to last 10 sts; (ch 1, skip next ch, sc in next st) 5 times: 121 sc and 120 chs. Finish off.

Row 3: With right side facing, join white with sc in first sc; *ch 1, skip next ch, sc in next sc; rep from * across. Finish off.

Second Half

Row 1: With right side facing and working in free lps on opposite edge of foundation ch, join lime with sc in first ch; ch 1, skip next ch, sc in next ch; rep from * to end on Row 1 of First Half.

Rows 2 and 3: Rep Rows 2 and 3 on First Half.

Strip B (Make 8)

First Half

With lilac, ch 205.

Row 1 (right side): Tr in 5th ch from hook (4 skipped chs count as first tr); *ch 1, skip next ch, tr in next ch; ch 1, skip next ch, dc in next ch; ch 1, skip next ch, hdc in next ch; ch 1, skip next ch, sc in next ch; (work CL, skip next ch, sc in next ch) twice;

ch 1, skip next ch, hdc in next ch; ch 1, skip next ch, dc in next ch; ch 1, skip next ch, tr in next ch; ch 1, skip next ch**; V-st in next ch; rep from * across to last 20 chs; rep from * to ** once; 2 tr in last ch: 30 sc, 20 hdc, 20 dc, 42 tr, 20 CL and 89 chs; ch 1, turn.

Note: Loop piece of contrasting yarn around last tr made to mark as right side and top edge.

Row 2: Keeping CL on right side, sc in first tr; ch 1, sc in next tr; (ch 1, skip next ch or CL, sc in next st) 10 times; *ch 1, sc in next ch; ch l, sc in next tr; (ch 1, skip next ch or CL, sc in next st) 10 times; rep from * across to last tr; ch 1, sc in last tr: 121 sc and 120 chs. Finish off.

Row 3: Rep Row 3 on First Half of Strip A.

Second Half

Row 1: With right side facing and working in free lps on opposite edge of foundation ch, join lilac with sl st in first ch; ch 4 (counts as first tr), tr in same ch as joining; rep from * to end on Row 1 of First Half of Strip B.

Rows 2 and 3: Rep Rows 2 and 3 on First Half of Strip B.

Assembly

Arrange strips with right sides facing in alternating sequence with Strip A on each outer edge and marked edges at top. With white, whip stitch strips together through both lps of each st on Row 3.

Edging

With right side facing, join white with sl st in first sc on Row 3 on left edge; sl st in next ch-1 sp; *ch 1, sl st in next ch-1 sp; rep from * across to last sc; sl st in last sc. Finish off. Rep on right edge.

Fringe

Following Single Knot Fringe Instructions on page 27, cut strands of each color 12" long. Hold afghan with short edges at top and bottom. Knot 2 strands of corresponding row color in edge of each st on top and bottom edges. **Note:** Knot three fringes in each tr and one fringe in each sc. Before tightening fringe, draw corresponding yarn end through fringe. Trim fringe.

Cluster Strips

Size: 34" x 45" plus fringe

MATERIALS

Sport weight yarn,
- 7 oz white
- 4 oz lime
- 5 oz blue
- 5 oz lilac
- 4 oz yellow

Note: Photographed model made with Red Heart® Soft Baby® #7001 White, #7624 Lime, #7822 Sky Blue, #7588 Lilac and #7321 Powder Yellow

Size G (4 mm) crochet hook (or size required for gauge)

GAUGE

5 Clusters = 4 3/4"

Strip = 1 5/8" wide x 45" long

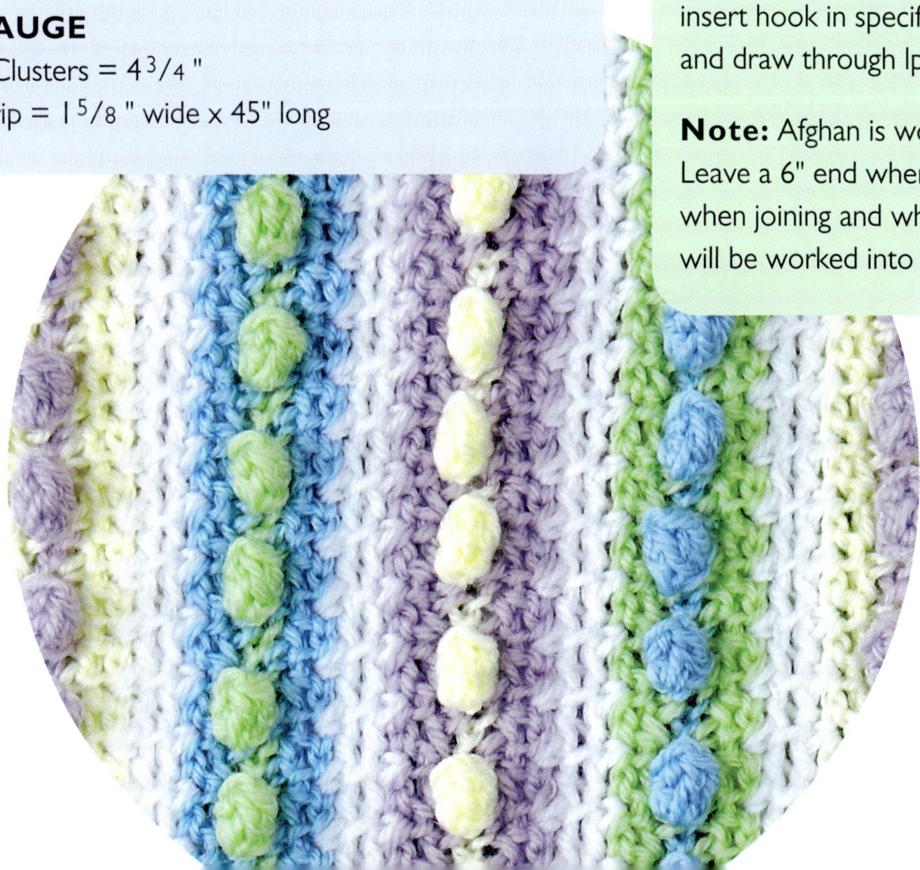

SPECIAL STITCHES

Cluster (CL): Sc in 2nd ch from hook, (2 dc, sc) in next ch (4-st row made); fold row in half from right to left, sl st in single lp at edge of first sc made: CL made.

To Join with Sl St: Place slip knot on hook, insert hook in specified st and draw up a lp, pull lp through slip knot.

To Join with Sc: Place slip knot on hook, insert hook in specified st and draw up a lp, YO and draw through lp on hook and slip knot.

Note: Afghan is worked in lengthwise rows. Leave a 6" end when starting foundation chain, when joining and when finishing off. These ends will be worked into fringe later.

Instructions

Strip A (make 6)

CL Row (right side):
With lime, ch 4, work CL; (ch 6, work CL) 46 times; ch 1: 47 CL and 140 chs. Finish off.

Note: Loop short piece of contrasting yarn around last CL made to mark as right side and top edge.

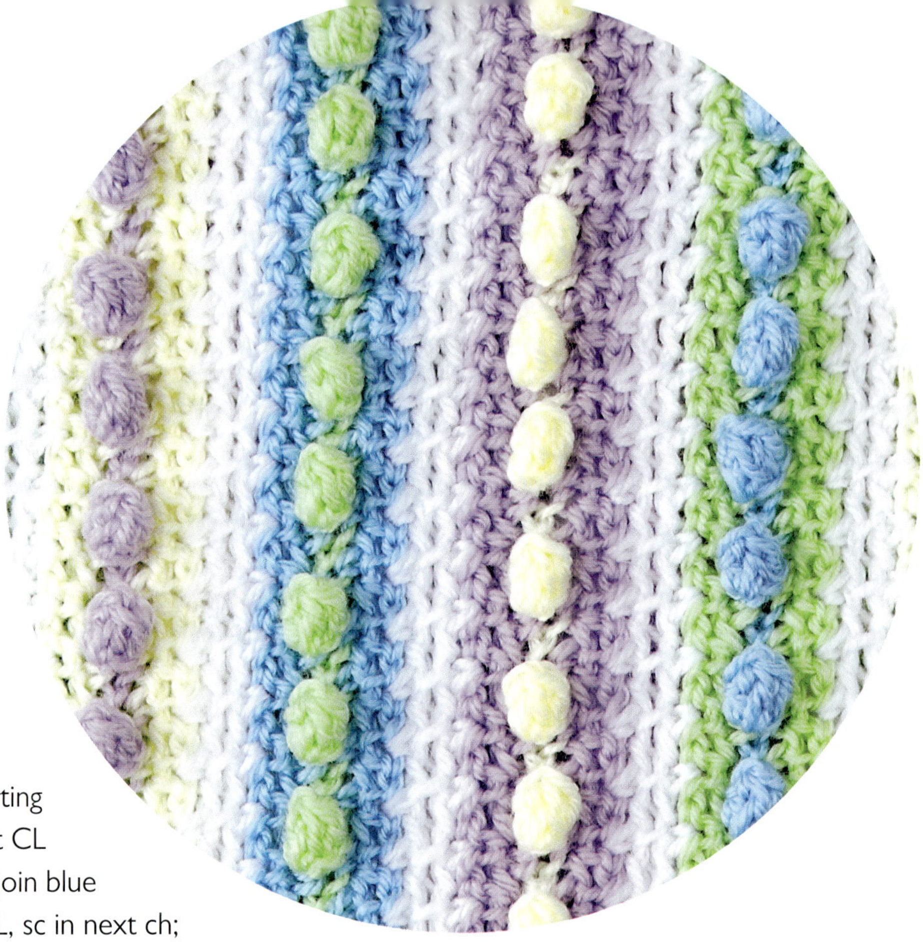

First Half

Row 1: With right side facing, starting at top edge, taking care not to twist CL Row and keeping CL on right side, join blue with sc in first ch; ch 1, skip next CL, sc in next ch; *ch 1, skip next ch, sc in next ch; ch 1, skip next CL, sc in next ch; rep from * across: 94 sc and 93 chs. Finish off.

Row 2: With wrong side facing, join blue with sc in first sc; *ch 1, skip next ch, sc in next sc; rep from * across. Finish off.

Row 3: With right side facing, join white with sc in first sc; rep Row 2 from * to end. Finish off.

Second Half

Row 1: With right side facing and working in free lps on opposite edge of CL Row, keeping CL on right side, join blue with sc in first ch; ch 1, skip next CL, sc in next ch; rep from * to end on Row 1 of First Half.

Rows 2 and 3: Rep Rows 2 and 3 on First Half.

Strip B (make 5)

Work same as Strip A, using lilac for Cluster Row, yellow for Rows 1 and 2 and white for Row 3.

Strip C (make 5)

Work same as Strip A, using blue for Cluster Row, lime for Rows 1 and 2 and white for Row 3.

Strip D (make 5)

Work same as Strip A, using yellow for Cluster Row, lilac for Rows 1 and 2 and white for Row 3.

Assembly

Arrange strips with right sides facing, alternating strips A, B, C and D in order, with Strip A on each outer edge and marked edges at top. With white, whip stitch strips together through both lps of each st on Row 3.

Edging

With right side facing, join white with sl st in first sc on Row 3 on left edge; sl st in next ch-1 sp; *ch 1, sl st in next ch-1 sp; rep from * across to last sc; sl st in last sc. Finish off. Rep on right edge.

Fringe

Following Single Knot Fringe Instructions on page 27, cut strands of each color 12" long. Hold afghan with short edges at top and bottom. Knot 2 strands of corresponding row color in edge of each st on top and bottom edges. Before tightening fringe, draw corresponding yarn end through fringe. Trim fringe.

Ripple Clusters

Size: 34" x 46" plus fringe

MATERIALS

Sport weight yarn,
24 oz pink print

Note: Photographed model made with Red Heart® Soft Baby® #7043 Tootsie Print

Size G (4 mm) crochet hook (or size required for gauge)

Size F (3.75 mm) crochet hook

GAUGE

With larger hook: (ch 1, dc) 5 times = 2 1/2"

SPECIAL STITCHES

To Join with Sl St: Place slip knot on hook, insert hook in specified st and draw up a lp, draw lp through slip knot.

To Join with Sc: Place slip knot on hook, insert hook in specified st and draw up a lp, YO and draw through lp on hook and slip knot.

Dc decrease (dc dec): YO, insert hook in first specified st and draw up a lp, YO and draw through 2 lps on hook; YO, insert hook in next specified st and draw up a lp, YO and draw through 2 lps on hook; YO and draw through all 3 lps on hook: dc dec made.

Bobble (BB): Ch 4, sc in 2nd ch from hook, dc in next ch; dc dec in same ch and in last ch (3-st row made); fold row in half from right to left, insert hook in single lp at edge of sc, insert hook in first ch of ch-4, YO and draw through all lps on hook, ch 1 tightly: BB made.

Note: Afghan is worked in lengthwise rows. Leave a 6" end when starting foundation chain, when joining and when finishing off. These ends will be worked into fringe later.

Instructions

With larger hook, ch 188.

Row 1 (wrong side): Dc in 6th ch from hook (5 skipped chs count as dc and ch-1 sp); (ch 1, skip next ch, dc in next ch) 4 times; (work BB, skip next ch, dc in next ch) twice; *(ch 1, skip next ch, dc in next ch) 5 times; (work BB, skip next ch, dc in next ch) twice; rep from * across to last 2 chs; ch 1, skip next ch, dc in last ch: 93 dc, 66 ch-1 sps and 26 BB; ch 3 (counts as dc and ch-1 sp on next row now and throughout), turn.

Note: Loop short piece of yarn around back of any st to mark as right side. Keep BB on right side now and throughout.

Row 2 (right side): Dc in next dc, ch 1, dc in next dc; (work BB, dc in next dc) twice; *(ch 1, dc in next dc) 5 times; (work BB, dc in next dc) twice; rep from * 11 times more; (ch 1, dc in next dc) 3 times; ch 1, skip next ch, dc in next ch; ch 3, turn.

Row 3: Dc in next dc; (ch 1, dc in next dc) twice; (work BB, dc in next dc) twice; *(ch 1, dc in next dc) 5 times; (work BB, dc in next dc) twice; rep from * 11 times more; (ch 1, dc in next dc) twice; ch 1, skip next ch, dc in next ch; ch 3, turn.

Row 4: Dc in next dc; (ch 1, dc in next dc) 3 times; (work BB, dc in next dc) twice; *(ch 1, dc in next dc) 5 times; (work BB, dc in next dc) twice; rep from * 11 times more; ch 1, dc in next dc; ch 1, skip next ch, dc in next ch; ch 3, turn.

Row 5: Dc in next dc; *(work BB, dc in next dc) twice**; (ch 1, dc in next dc) 5 times; rep from * 11 times more; rep from * to ** once; (ch 1, dc in next dc) 4 times; ch 1, skip next ch, dc in next ch; ch 3, turn.

Row 6: Rep Row 4.

Row 7: Rep Row 3.

Row 8: Rep Row 2.

Row 9: Dc in next dc; (ch 1, dc in next dc) 4 times; (work BB, dc in next dc) twice; *(ch 1, dc in next dc) 5 times; (work BB, dc in next dc) twice; rep from * 11 times more; ch 1, skip next ch, dc in next ch; ch 3, turn.

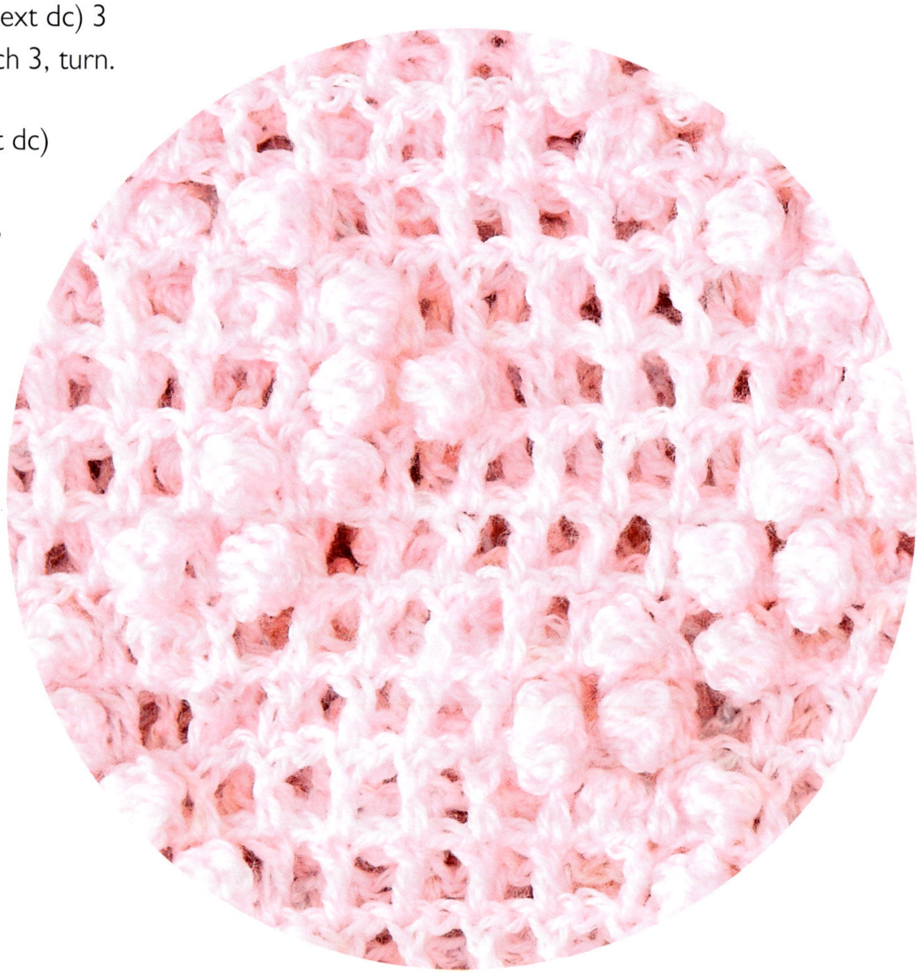

Rows 10 through 65: Rep Rows 2 through 9 seven times more.

Row 66: Dc in next dc; *ch 1, dc in next dc; rep from * across to turning ch; ch 1, skip next ch, dc in 2nd ch of turning ch-3: 93 dc and 92 ch-1 sps; ch 3, turn.

Row 67: Rep Row 66, except ch 1 at end instead of ch 3. Do not finish off.

Top Edging

Row 1: Sc in first dc, sc in next ch (not in ch-1 sp); *ch 1, skip next dc, sc in next ch; rep from * across to last 2 chs; sc in 2nd ch of turning ch-3: 94 sc and 91 ch-1 sps. Finish off.

Row 2: With right side facing and smaller hook, join with sl st in first sc; ch 2, skip next sc; *sl st in next ch-1 sp, ch 2, skip next sc; rep from * across to last sc; sl st in last sc: 93 sl sts and 92 ch-2 sps. Finish off.

Bottom Edging

Row 1: With right side facing and larger hook, working in 2 lps of chs on foundation ch, join with sc in 4th skipped ch at beg of Row 1, sc in 5th skipped ch; *ch 1, skip ch at base of next dc, sc in next ch; rep from * across to last ch; sc in ch at base of last dc: 94 sc and 91 ch-1 sps. Finish off.

Row 2: Rep Row 2 of Edging.

Fringe

Following Single Knot Fringe Instructions on page 27, cut 12" long strands. Hold afghan with short edges at top and bottom. Knot 4 strands around edge of each row and in each edging on top and bottom edges. Before tightening fringe, draw corresponding yarn end through fringe. Trim fringe.

Alternating Bobbles

Size: 34" x 45" plus fringe

MATERIALS

Sport weight yarn,
14 oz multicolor
21 oz mint

Note: Photographed model made with Red Heart® Soft Baby® # 7973 Seashore and #7680 Mint

Size G (4 mm) crochet hook (or size required for gauge)

Size F (3.75 mm) crochet hook

GAUGE

With larger hook, 12 sts = 3 1/4"

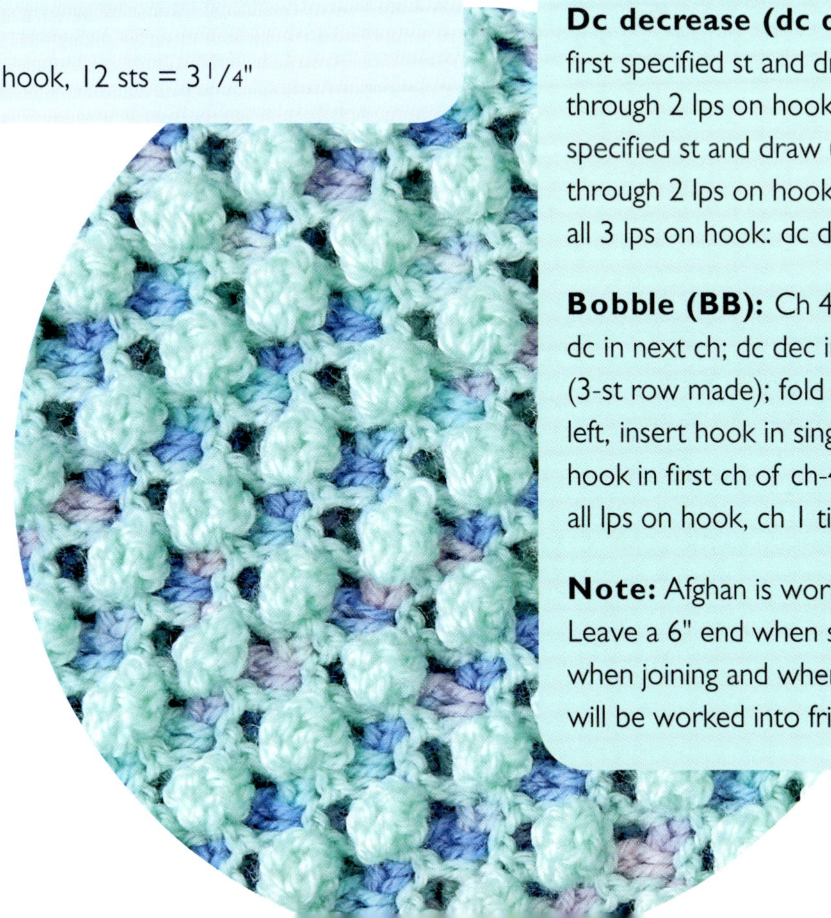

SPECIAL STITCHES

To Join with Sl St: Place slip knot on hook, insert hook in specified st and draw up a lp, draw lp through slip knot.

To Join with Sc: Place slip knot on hook, insert hook in specified st and draw up a lp, YO and draw through lp on hook and slip knot.

To Join with Dc: Place slip knot on hook, YO; holding slip knot and YO with index finger, insert hook in specified st and draw up a lp, YO and draw through 2 lps on hook, YO and draw through lp on hook and slip knot.

Dc decrease (dc dec): YO, insert hook in first specified st and draw up a lp, YO and draw through 2 lps on hook; YO, insert hook in next specified st and draw up a lp, YO and draw through 2 lps on hook; YO and draw through all 3 lps on hook: dc dec made.

Bobble (BB): Ch 4, sc in 2nd ch from hook, dc in next ch; dc dec in same ch and in last ch (3-st row made); fold row in half from right to left, insert hook in single lp at edge of sc, insert hook in first ch of ch-4, YO and draw through all lps on hook, ch 1 tightly: BB made.

Note: Afghan is worked in lengthwise rows. Leave a 6" end when starting foundation ch, when joining and when finishing off. These ends will be worked into fringe later.

Instructions

Body

With multicolor, ch 168.

Row 1 (right side): Sc in 2nd ch from hook; *ch 1, skip next ch, sc in next ch; rep from * across: 84 sc and 83 ch-1 sps. Finish off.

Note: Loop short piece of yarn around any st to mark Row 1 as right side.

Row 2: With wrong side facing, join mint with dc in first sc; work BB; skip next st, dc in next sc; *ch 1, skip next st, dc in next sc; work BB; skip next st, dc in next sc; rep from * across: 84 dc, 42 BB and 41 ch-1 sps. Finish off.

Row 3: With right side facing, join multicolor with sc in first dc; working behind next BB, tr in ch-1 sp one row below BB, sc in next dc; *ch 1, sc in next dc; working behind next BB, tr in ch-l sp one row below BB, sc in next dc; rep from * across: 84 sc, 42 tr and 41 ch-1 sps. Finish off.

Row 4: With wrong side facing, join mint with dc in first sc; ch 1, skip next st, dc in next sc; *work BB; skip next st, dc in next sc; ch 1, skip next st, dc in next sc; rep from * across: 84 dc, 41 BB and 42 ch-1 sps. Finish off.

Row 5: With right side facing, join multicolor with sc in first dc; ch 1, sc in next dc; *working behind next BB, tr in ch-1 sp one row below BB, sc in next dc; ch 1, sc in next dc; rep from * across: 84 sc, 41 tr and 42 ch-1 sps. Finish off.

Rep Rows 2 through 5 until afghan measures about 32" from beg, then rep Rows 2 and 3 once more.

Top Edging

Row 1: With wrong side facing and larger hook, join multicolor with sc in first sc on last row; *ch 1, skip next st, sc in next sc; rep from * across: 84 sc and 83 ch-1 sps. Finish off.

Row 2: With right side facing and smaller hook, join multicolor with sl st in first sc; sl st in next ch-1 sp; *ch 2, sl st in next ch-1 sp; rep from * across to last sc; sl st in last sc: 85 sl sts and 82 ch-2 sps. Finish off.

Bottom Edging

With right side facing and F hook, working in free lps and ch-1 sps of foundation ch, join multicolor with sl st in first ch; sl st in next ch-1 sp; *ch 2, sl st in next ch-1 sp; rep from * across to last ch; sl st in last ch: 85 sl sts and 82 ch-2 sps. Finish off.

Fringe

Following Single Knot Fringe Instructions on page 27, cut strands of each color 12" long. Hold afghan with short edges at top and bottom. Knot 2 strands of corresponding row color in edge of each st on top and bottom edges.

Note: Knot two fringes in each dc and one fringe in each sc. Before tightening fringe, draw corresponding yarn end through fringe. Trim fringe.

Cluster Blocks

Instructions begin on next page.

Cluster Blocks

Size: 34 1/2" x 45 1/2" plus fringe

MATERIALS

Sport weight yarn,
23 oz multicolor

Note: Photographed model made with Red Heart® Soft Baby® #7915 Koolaid

Size G (4 mm) crochet hook
(or size required for gauge)

Size F (3.75 mm) crochet hook

GAUGE

With larger hook, 13 dc = 3 1/2"

SPECIAL STITCHES:

Dc decrease (dc dec): YO, insert hook in first specified st and draw up a lp, YO and draw through 2 lps on hook; YO, insert hook in next specified st and draw up a lp, YO and draw through 2 lps on hook; YO and draw through all 3 lps on hook: dc dec made.

Bobble (BB): Ch 4, sc in 2nd ch from hook, dc in next ch; dc dec in same ch and in last ch (3-st row made); fold row in half from right to left, insert hook in single lp at edge of sc, insert hook in first ch of ch-4, YO and draw through all lps on hook, ch 1 tightly: BB made.

To Join with Sc: Place slip knot on hook, insert hook in specified st and draw up a lp, YO and draw through lp on hook and slip knot.

Note: Afghan is worked in lengthwise rows. Leave a 6" end when starting foundation chain, when joining and when finishing off. These ends will be worked into fringe later.

Instructions

With larger hook, ch 171.

Row 1 (wrong side): Dc in 4th ch from hook (3 skipped sts count at first dc), dc in next ch and in each rem ch across: 169 dc; ch 2 (counts as dc on next row now and throughout), turn.

Note: Loop short piece of yarn around back of any st to mark as right side.

Row 2 (right side): Dc in next dc and in each rem dc across, working last dc in first skipped ch at beg of Row 1; ch 2, turn.

Row 3: Dc in next 3 dc; *ch 1, skip next st, dc in next dc; (work BB, skip next st, dc in next dc) twice; ch 1, skip next st, dc in next 4 dc; rep from * across, working last dc in 2nd ch of turning ch-2: 109 dc, 30 chs and 30 BB; ch 2, turn.

Note: Keep BB on right side now and throughout.

Row 4: Rep Row 3.

Rows 5 and 6: Dc in next 3 dc; *(ch 1, skip next st, dc in next dc) 3 times; ch 1, skip next st, dc in next 4 dc; rep from * across, working last dc in 2nd ch of turning ch-2: 109 dc and 60 chs; ch 2, turn.

Row 7: Dc in next 3 dc; *(dc in next ch [not in ch-1 sp], dc in next dc) 4 times; dc in next 3 dc; rep from * across, working last dc in 2nd ch of turning ch-2: 169 dc; ch 2, turn.

Row 8: Dc in next dc and in each rem dc across, working last dc in 2nd ch of turning ch-2; ch 2, turn.

Rep Rows 3 through 8 until afghan measures about 34". At end of last row, ch 1, turn instead of ch 2, turn. Do not finish off.

Top Edging

Row 1: Sc in first 2 dc; *ch 1, skip next dc, sc in next dc; rep from * across to turning ch, sc in 2nd ch of turning ch-2: 86 sc and 83 ch-1 sps; ch 1, turn.

Row 2: With smaller hook, sl st in first sc; *ch 2, skip next sc, sl st in next ch-1 sp; rep from * across to last 2 sc; ch 2, skip next sc, sl st in last sc: 85 sl sts and 84 ch-2 sps. Finish off.

Bottom Edging

Row 1: With wrong side facing and larger hook, working in free lps of foundation ch, join with sc in first ch, sc in next ch; *ch 1, skip next ch, sc in next ch; rep from * across to last ch; sc in last ch (3rd skipped ch at beg of Row 1): 86 sc and 83 ch-1 sps; ch 1, turn.

Row 2: Rep Row 2 of Edging.

Fringe

Following Single Knot Fringe Instructions on page 27, cut 12" long strands. Hold afghan with short edges at top and bottom. Knot 4 strands around edge of each row and in each edging on top and bottom edges. Before tightening fringe, draw corresponding yarn end through fringe. Trim fringe.

Cluster Stripes

Size: 34" x 45" plus fringe

MATERIALS

Sport weight yarn,
 21 oz yellow
 6 oz blue
 6 oz multicolor

Note: Photographed model made with Red Heart® Soft Baby® #7321 Powder Yellow, #7822 Sky Blue and #8889 Laddie Print

Size G (4 mm) crochet hook (or size required for gauge)

GAUGE

13 sts = 3"

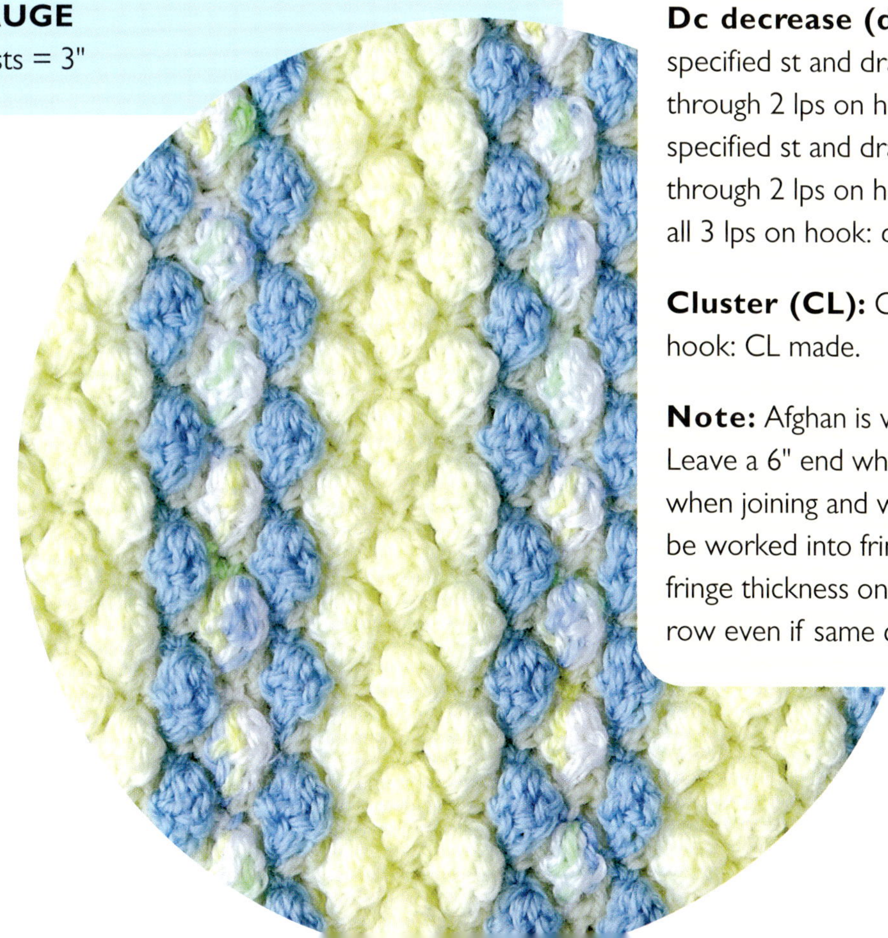

SPECIAL STITCHES

To Join with Sl St: Place slip knot on hook, insert hook in specified st and draw up a lp, pull lp through slip knot.

To Join with Sc: Place slip knot on hook, insert hook in specified st and draw up a lp, YO and draw through lp on hook and slip knot.

Dc decrease (dc dec): YO, insert hook in specified st and draw up a lp, YO and draw through 2 lps on hook; YO, insert hook in next specified st and draw up a lp, YO and draw through 2 lps on hook; YO and draw through all 3 lps on hook: dc dec made.

Cluster (CL): Ch 3; dc dec in 3rd ch from hook: CL made.

Note: Afghan is worked in lengthwise rows. Leave a 6" end when starting foundation ch, when joining and when finishing off. These ends be worked into fringe later. To maintain same fringe thickness on both ends, finish off each row even if same color continues on next row.

Instructions

With yellow, ch 194.

Row 1 (right side): Sc in 2nd ch from hook; (ch 1, skip next ch, sc in next ch; rep from * across: 97 sc and 96 chs. Finish off.

Note: Loop short piece of contrasting yarn around any st to mark Row 1 as right side.

Row 2: With wrong side facing, join blue with sc in first sc; *work CL; ch 1, skip next 3 sts, sc in next st; rep from * across: 49 sc, 48 CL and 48 chs. Finish off.

Row 3: With right side facing, join yellow with sc in first sc; *ch 1; working behind next CL, dc in skipped sc one row below CL; ch 1, sc in next sc on previous row; rep from * across: 49 sc, 48 dc and 96 chs. Finish off.

Row 4: With wrong side facing, join multicolor with sc in first sc; ch 1, skip next ch, sc in next dc; *work CL; ch 1, skip next 3 sts, sc in next st; rep from * across to last 2 sts; ch 1, skip next ch, sc in last sc: 50 sc, 47 CL and 49 chs. Finish off.

Row 5: With right side facing, join yellow with sc in first sc; ch 1, skip next ch, sc in next sc; *ch 1; working behind next CL, dc in skipped sc one row below CL; ch 1, sc in next sc on previous row; rep from * across to last 2 sts; ch 1, skip next ch, sc in last sc: 50 sc, 47 dc and 96 chs. Finish off.

Rows 6 and 7: Rep Rows 2 and 3.

Rows 8 and 9: With yellow, rep Rows 4 and 5.

Rows 10 through 13: With yellow, rep Rows 2 through 5.

Rep Rows 2 through 13 until afghan measures about 32", then rep Rows 2 through 7 once more.

Top Edging

Row 1: With wrong side facing, join yellow with sc in first sc; *ch 1, skip next ch, sc in next st; rep from * across: 97 sc and 96 ch-1 sps. Finish off.

Row 2: With right side facing, join yellow with sl st in first sc; sl st in next ch-1 sp; *ch 1, skip next sc, sl st in next ch-1 sp; rep from * across to last sc; sl st in last sc: 98 sl sts and 95 chs. Finish off.

Bottom Edging

With right side facing and working in free lps and ch-1 sps of foundation ch, join yellow with sl st in first ch; sl st in next ch-1 sp; *ch 1, sl st in next ch-1 sp; rep from * across to last ch; sl st in last ch: 98 sl sts and 95 chs. Finish off.

Fringe

Following Single Knot Fringe Instructions on page 27, cut strands of each color 12" long. Hold afghan with short edges at top and bottom. Knot 2 strands of corresponding row color in edge of every other row on top and bottom edges. Before tightening fringe, draw corresponding yarn end through fringe. Trim fringe.

General Directions

Crochet patterns are written in a special shorthand which is used so that instructions don't take up too much space. They sometimes seem confusing, but once you learn them, you'll have no trouble following them.

Abbreviations

BB	bobble
Beg	beginning
Cl(s)	cluster(s)
Ch(s)	chain(s)
Dc	double crochet
Dc dec	double crochet decrease
Hdc	half double crochet
Inc	Increase(ing)
Lp(s)	loop(s)
Mm	millimeters
Oz	ounces
Prev	previous
Rem	remaining
Rep	repeat(ing)
Sc	single crochet
Sl st	slip stitch
Sp(s)	space(s)
St(s)	stitch(es)
Tog	together
Tr	triple crochet
V-st	V-stitch
YO	yarn over hook

Standard Symbols

*An asterisk (or double asterisks**) in a pattern row, indicates a portion of instructions to be used more than once. For instance, "rep from * three times" means that after working the instructions once, you must work them again three times for a total of 4 times in all.

: The number of stitches after a colon tells you the number of stitches you will have when you have completed the row.

( ) Parentheses enclose instructions which are to be worked the number of times following the parentheses. For instance, "(ch 1, sc, ch 1) 3 times" means that you will chain one, work one sc, and then chain again three times for a total of six chains and three sc's.

Parentheses often set off or clarify a group of stitches to be worked into the same space or stitch. For instance, "(dc, ch 2, dc) in corner sp".

[ ] Brackets and ( ) parentheses are also used to give you additional information.

Terms

Join — This means to join with a sl st unless another stitch is specified.

Finish Off — This means to end your piece by pulling the cut yarn end through the last loop remaining on the hook. This will prevent the work from unraveling.

Continue in Pattern as Established — This means to follow the pattern stitch as it has been set up, working any increases or decreases in such a way that the pattern remains the same as it was established.

Work even — This means that the work is continued in the pattern as established without increasing or decreasing.

Term Equivalents

The patterns in this book have been written using the crochet terminology that is used in the United States. Terms which may have different equivalents in other parts of the world are listed below.

United States	International
Double crochet (dc)	treble crochet (tr)
Gauge	tension
Half double crochet (hdc)	half treble crochet (htr)
Single crochet	double crochet
Skip	miss
Slip stitch	single crochet
Triple crochet (tr)	double treble crochet (dtr)
Yarn over (YO)	yarn forward (yfwd)
Yarn over (YO)	Yarn around needle (yrn)

CROCHET HOOKS CONVERSION CHART

U.S.	B-1	C-2	D-3	E-4	F-5	G-6	H-8	I-9	J-10	K-10 1/2	N	P	Q
Metric	2.25	2.75	3.25	3.5	3.75	4	5	5.5	6	6.5	9	10	15

Gauge

This is probably the most important aspect of crocheting!

GAUGE simply means the number of stitches per inch, and the numbers of rows per inch that result from a specified yarn worked with a hook in a specified size. But since everyone knits or crochets differently-some loosely, some tightly, some in between-the measurements of individual work can vary greatly, even when the crocheters use the same pattern and the same size yarn and hook.

If you don't work to the gauge specified in the pattern, your afghan will never be the correct size, and you may not have enough yarn to finish your project. The hook size given in the instructions is merely a guide and should never be used without a gauge swatch.

To make a gauge swatch, crochet a swatch that is about 4" square, using the suggested hook and the number of stitches given in the pattern. Measure your swatch. If the number of stitches is fewer than those listed in the pattern, try making another swatch with a smaller hook. If the number of stitches is more than is called for in the pattern, try making another swatch with a larger hook. It is your responsibility to make sure you achieve the gauge specified in the pattern.

Fringe

Cut a piece of cardboard about 6" wide and half as long as specified in the instructions for strands, plus 1/2" for trimming allowance. Wind the yarn loosely and evenly lengthwise around the cardboard. When the card is filled, cut the yarn across one end. Do this several times; then begin fringing. You can wind additional strands as you need them.

1. Hold the specified number of strands for one knot of fringe together, and then fold in half.

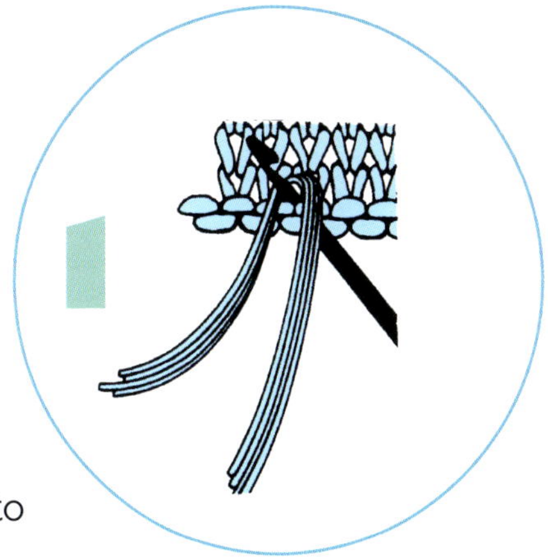

2. Hold the project with the right side facing you. Using a crochet hook, draw the folded ends through the space of stitch from right to wrong side.

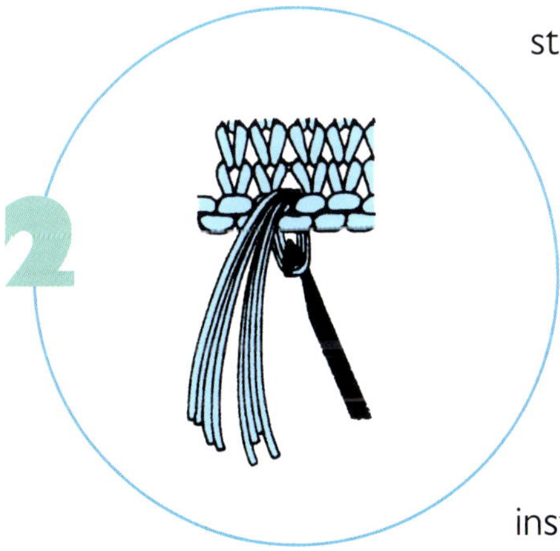

3. Pull the loose ends through the folded section.

4. Draw the knot up firmly.

Space the knots as indicated in the pattern instructions. Trim the ends of the fringe evenly.

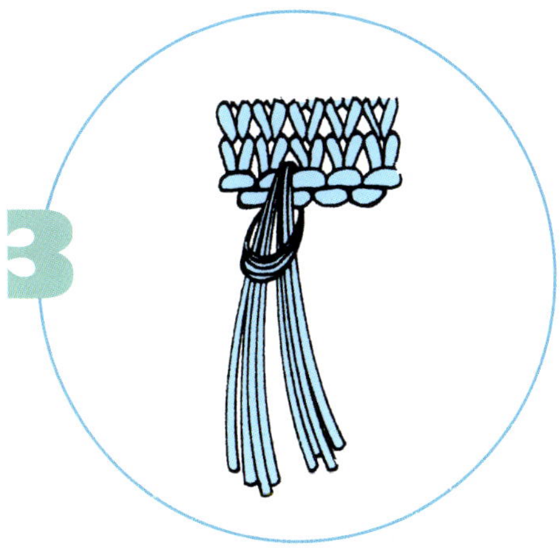

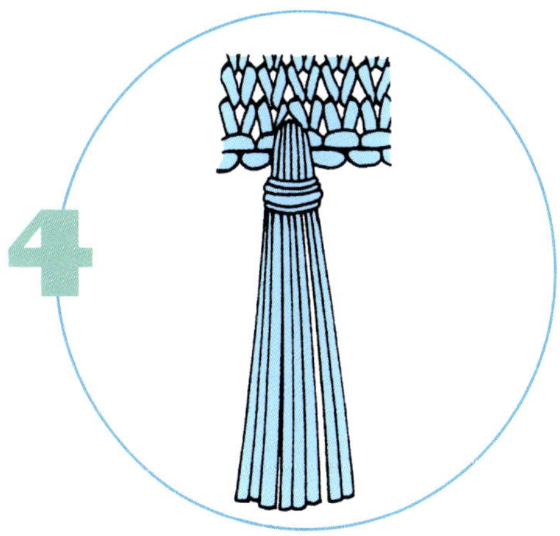

Managing Editor
Susan Lowman

Book Design
Joyce Lerner

Produced by The Creative Partners™, LLC

The yarn for these afghans was supplied by Coats and Clark. If you are unable to find the yarns locally, write to the manufacturer who will be able to tell you where to purchase their products, or consult their internet sites:
Coats and Clark
Consumer Services
P.O. Box 12229
Greenville, South Carolina 29612-0229
www.coatsandclark.com

All of the afghans in this book were tested to ensure the accuracy and clarity of the instructions.
We are grateful to the following pattern testers:
Carrie Cristiano
Wilma Keith
Jennifer Marr
Marjorie Scensny
Marsha Seiber
Carole Sullivan

Every effort has been made to ensure the accuracy of these instructions.
We cannot be responsible for human error or variations in your work.

ISBN# 1-60140-087-X